# ANIMAL ATTACK!

# Hunting with KOMODO DRAGONS

By Max Maimone

**Gareth Stevens**
Publishing

**Please visit our website, www.garethstevens.com. For a free color catalog of all our high-quality books, call toll free 1-800-542-2595 or fax 1-877-542-2596.**

**Library of Congress Cataloging-in-Publication Data**

Maimone, Max.
Hunting with komodo dragons / by Max Maimone.
  p. cm. — (Animal attack!)
Includes index.
ISBN 978-1-4824-0498-2 (pbk.)
ISBN 978-1-4824-0514-9 (6-pack)
ISBN 978-1-4824-0497-5 (library binding)
1. Komodo dragon — Juvenile literature. I. Title.
QL666.L29 M35 2014
597.95—dc23

First Edition

Published in 2014 by
**Gareth Stevens Publishing**
111 East 14th Street, Suite 349
New York, NY 10003

Copyright © 2014 Gareth Stevens Publishing

Designer: Katelyn E. Reynolds
Editor: Therese Shea

Photo credits: Cover, p. 1 (cover, pp. 1, 3–24 background image) Anna Kucherova/Shutterstock.com; cover, pp. 1, 3–24 (background graphic) pashabo/Shutterstock.com; cover, pp. 4–23 (splatter graphic) jgl247/Shutterstock.com; p. 5 Kevin Lings/Shutterstock.com; p. 6 Hemera Technologies/PhotoObjects.net/Thinkstock.com; p. 7 (map) Volina/Shutterstock.com; pp. 7 (main), 18 Ethan Daniels/Shutterstock.com; p. 9 Marvin E. Newman/Photographer's Choice/Getty Images; p. 10 David Evison/Shutterstock.com; pp. 11, 19 Reinhard Dirscherl/WaterFrame/Getty Images; p. 13 Sergey Uryadnikov/Shutterstock.com; p. 15 Bronson Chang/Shutterstock.com; p. 17 Scott Barbour/Getty Images; p. 21 Peter Macdiarmid/Getty Images.

Printed in the United States of America

CPSIA compliance information: Batch #CW14GS: For further information contact Gareth Stevens, New York, New York at 1-800-542-2595.

# CONTENTS

Words in the glossary appear in **bold** type
the first time they are used in the text.

# HUNGRY FOR MEAT

The deer chomps on grass as the sun goes down. It looks up to make sure there's no danger near. It hears something. Out of the bushes darts a very large lizard with long claws and sharp teeth. It's a hungry Komodo dragon!

Komodo dragons are the heaviest lizards in the world. Males can weigh 300 pounds (136 kg) and reach lengths of 10 feet (3 m)! Most lizards eat all kinds of food, but not Komodo dragons. They're only hungry for meat!

## Fact Hunter

Komodo dragons are a kind of monitor lizard. Monitor lizards first roamed Earth over 100 million years ago, when dinosaurs were still alive!

Female Komodo dragons are smaller than males.

# LITTLE DRAGONS

Komodo dragons really do look like dragons. They have a long head, round **snout**, four short legs, and a long, strong tail. Lizards are reptiles, and like other reptiles, Komodo dragons have scaly skin. It's a muddy green color. That's helpful because they like to sit and wait for their prey to walk by. Their skin acts as **camouflage**.

If Komodo dragons sound a bit scary, you don't have to worry. They're only found on a few **tropical** islands in Indonesia.

The Komodo dragon got its name from one
of its island homes—Komodo Island.

# TASTING TONGUE

Perhaps another reason why Komodo dragons look like dragons in storybooks is their tongue. It's long, yellow, and **forked**. Komodo dragons often stick out their tongue, making them look a bit like dragons breathing fire.

When a Komodo dragon draws its tongue back into its mouth, a special body part "smells" what was in the air. Depending on where on the tongue the smell was found, the lizard can even tell in what direction prey may be!

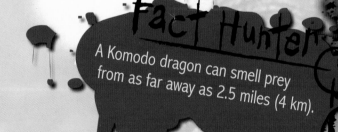

Fact Hunter

A Komodo dragon can smell prey from as far away as 2.5 miles (4 km).

The body part that helps a Komodo dragon smell with its tongue is called the Jacobson's organ.

# WHAT'S FOR DINNER?

Komodo dragons eat any kind of meat, alive or dead. They eat deer, pigs, water buffalo, snakes, fish, rats, mice, and even other Komodo dragons. They also eat carrion, which is an animal that's already dead.

Each Komodo dragon has about 60 sharp teeth to tear its prey apart. Its jaws are very strong and its throat is wide, so it can swallow big chunks of meat at a time. Komodo dragons can eat more than half their weight in one meal!

After a big meal, a Komodo dragon can go weeks before eating again.

# DEADLY BITE

How does a Komodo dragon take down prey that's bigger and heavier, like water buffalo? It has a terrible bite.

Komodo dragons can run fast for a short distance, about as fast as a dog. They bite their prey and then sometimes let it run away! Why? Because a Komodo dragon's spit contains deadly **venom**. The prey may escape, but it will finally die from the bite. The Komodo dragon sometimes just slowly follows behind and waits.

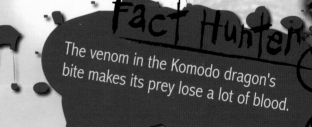

Fact Hunter

The venom in the Komodo dragon's bite makes its prey lose a lot of blood.

A Komodo dragon's bite isn't deadly to another Komodo dragon. Scientists are trying to figure out why.

▽

# A DAY WITH A DRAGON

Komodo dragons hunt during the day and stay in dens at night. When the sun rises, they lie in its light to raise their body temperature. Then they begin to hunt. During the hottest parts of the day, the Komodo dragon may need to cool down, so it lies in the shade. When the sun goes down, it heads back to its den.

Komodo dragons like to live alone. However, they may gather to eat prey together. The largest males always eat first.

Fact Hunter

Komodo dragons like to knock their prey down so they have a better chance to bite them.

Like other reptiles, Komodo dragons are cold-blooded. That means their body temperature changes with their surroundings.

# YOUNG DRAGONS

Mother Komodo dragons dig nests in the ground. They lay 15 to 30 eggs each September. The mother may **incubate** the eggs until they hatch about 9 months later. After that, though, the baby Komodo dragons are on their own!

Other animals—including adult Komodo dragons—like to eat baby Komodo dragons. So, the babies run up trees where many predators can't follow. They stay in the trees about 4 years, eating bugs, eggs, snakes, birds, and other small creatures.

Fact Hunter

Mother Komodo dragons may take over bird nests on the ground for their eggs.

Newly hatched Komodo dragons may
be about 1 foot (30 cm) long.

# WATCH OUT!

Komodo dragons sometimes attack people. Only a few people have died from attacks over the years, though. Still, people living on the same islands as Komodo dragons have to be careful.

It's illegal to kill or hunt Komodo dragons, but some people still do, to keep them from attacking their livestock. People also take over Komodo dragon territory for farms, buildings, and homes. Special lands have been set aside for Komodo dragons, such as Komodo National Park.

KOMODO NATIONAL PARK
Indonesia

THE WORLD HERITAGE SITE

There are many more male Komodo dragons than females, about four times as many.

A park ranger keeps his distance as he tries to get a Komodo dragon to move away from the beach.

19

# ENDANGERED

Komodo dragons are **endangered** and have been guarded by laws for many years. There are between 3,000 and 5,000 left.

Because Komodo dragons eat carrion, they play the important role in nature of "cleaning up" the leftovers of other animals. Though Komodo dragons are dangerous predators, people go to zoos and even all the way to Indonesia to see them. Komodo dragons draw many **tourists** to the islands every year. Would you want to see one?

Just don't get too close!

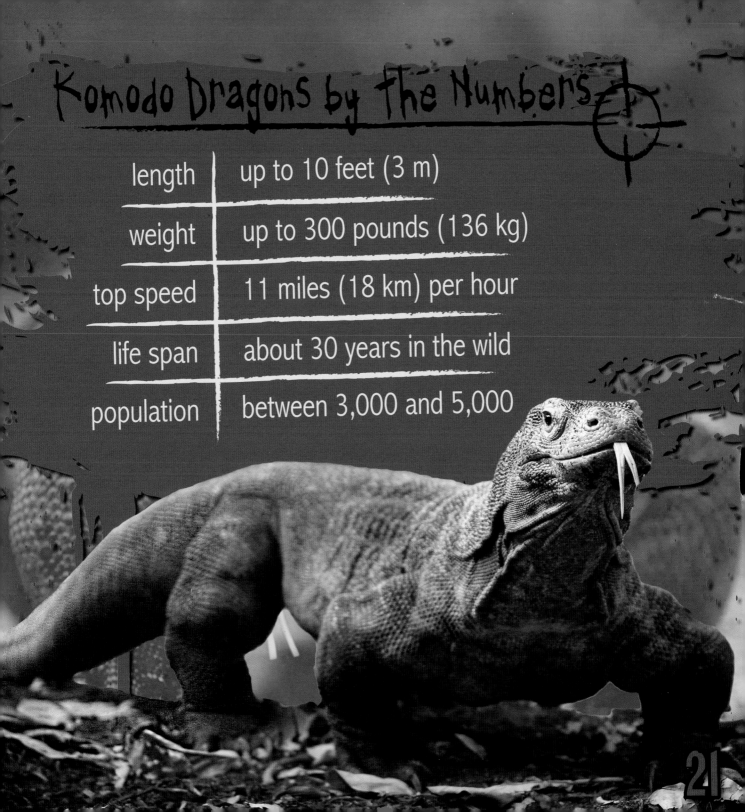

# Komodo Dragons by the Numbers

| | |
|---|---|
| length | up to 10 feet (3 m) |
| weight | up to 300 pounds (136 kg) |
| top speed | 11 miles (18 km) per hour |
| life span | about 30 years in the wild |
| population | between 3,000 and 5,000 |

# GLOSSARY

**camouflage:** animals' colors or shapes that allow them to blend with their surroundings

**endangered:** in danger of dying out

**forked:** divided into two parts

**incubate:** to keep eggs warm so they can hatch

**snout:** an animal's nose and mouth

**tourist:** one who visits places away from home for pleasure

**tropical:** having to do with the warm parts of Earth near the equator

**venom:** something an animal makes in its body that can harm other animals

# FOR MORE INFORMATION

## Books

Bjorklund, Ruth. *Komodo Dragons*. New York, NY: Children's Press, 2012.

Gish, Melissa. *Komodo Dragons*. Mankato, MN: Creative Education, 2012.

Miller, Geoff. *Komodo Dragons*. Danbury, CT: Grolier, 2009.

## Websites

**Komodo Dragon**
*nationalzoo.si.edu/animals/reptilesamphibians/facts/factsheets/Komododragon.cfm*
Find out more about Komodo dragons.

**Reptiles: Komodo Dragon**
*animals.sandiegozoo.org/animals/komodo-dragon*
Read more about the "king of the lizards."

# INDEX